MANNING UP
In the Face of Death

GREGG MANNING

WESTBOW°
PRESS
A DIVISION OF THOMAS NELSON
& ZONDERVAN

Scripture taken from the New King James Version unless otherwise noted. Copyright © 1982 by Thomas Nelson, Inc.

WestBow Press books may be ordered through booksellers or by contacting:

WestBow Press
A Division of Thomas Nelson & Zondervan
1663 Liberty Drive
Bloomington, IN 47403
www.westbowpress.com
1 (866) 928-1240

ISBN: 978-1-4908-4266-0 (sc)
ISBN: 978-1-4908-4267-7 (hc)
ISBN: 978-1-4908-4268-4 (e)

Library of Congress Control Number: 2014911524

Printed in the United States of America.

WestBow Press rev. date: 07/24/2014

CONTENTS

Acknowledgments ix

Introduction xi

Chapter 1   In the Beginning 1

Chapter 2   My Gethsemane 6

Chapter 3   Reality Sets In 11

Chapter 4   The Good, the Bad, and the Ugly 17

Chapter 5   Transformation 24

Chapter 6   Not If, but When 36

Chapter 7   Caregivers 41

Chapter 8   In the Zone 46

Chapter 9   Come to Me 52

Chapter 10   The Mystery Man 56

Chapter 11   The Four C's 60

Chapter 12   Forced Fasting 65

Chapter 13   He's Up! 69

Chapter 14   Jehovah Jireh 75

Chapter 15   Small Talk 82

Chapter 16   Facts of Life 86

Epilogue 91

Words to Live By 95

About the Author 97

Dedicated to the kindred spirits
who have stood at the precipice
and battled on.

Acknowledgments

I would be remiss if I didn't recognize the incredible personnel at the Texas Oncology clinic in Medical City. In particular, I'd like to thank Dr. Vikas Bhushan, a no-nonsense, get-after-it doctor who devised the success equation for my survival; his right hand and PA, Jennifer Potter, very thorough and always so positive, who always made me feel at ease no matter what my condition; and the litany of nurses and technicians at both hospitals who treated me as though I was their only patient. I am eternally grateful to all of you.

Introduction

I am just an ordinary man, but I have an extraordinary, God-inspired story to tell. It is a demonstration of the Holy Spirit's power. It's one reason why I tell it—in the hopes that your faith doesn't rest on man's conventional wisdom but on God's omnipotence. I also tell this story on behalf of those who have passed on as a result of cancer, on behalf of those who are too weak to tell their stories because of the cancer battle in which they are immersed, and for those who will find themselves in the middle of a cancer griddle in the future.

Any trials, tribulations, or even injustices that you may encounter in this life are offset by your freedom to choose your destiny in the next. I never, nor will I ever, question the fairness of what happened to me. I want to encourage you, no matter what your faith experience has been, to never turn your back on God. No matter what happens to you, tell Him that you will always love Him, if for nothing else than all of the days He has allowed you to open your eyes and breathe. If you have faith, you'll have a better future, and if you believe you'll have a better future, you'll have power in the present.

I know there is a Godly reason that I'm still alive. I am going to do my best, with however much time I have left, to make a difference on His behalf because I believe the expression "to him whom much has been given, much is expected." I thank God that His Spirit brought and continues to bring new life to my body and soul. I placed my life in His hands and my hope in His faithfulness and love. In the hospitals, I knew I never was alone, even in the small hours of the morning when it was so quiet I could have heard a pin drop. I knew God was with me. I could *feel* His presence.

Nevertheless, there were times when I felt as though I was in solitary confinement. I started to appreciate the isolation because during those uninterrupted times, I had unparalleled quiet time with the Lord. They became some of my most cherished times. When I needed extra courage during some intense battles, He dug a foxhole in my heart and jumped into it with me. To paraphrase 2 Corinthians 4:8–9, I was afflicted in a very serious way, but I wasn't crushed; I had been struck down, but I wasn't destroyed. I have to admit that I was perplexed, but I wasn't driven to despair.

My personal relationship with the Lord grew, and my faith began to soar. There was no way that I was going to walk the cancer path without Him, and no matter what we ran into on that path, I relied on Him to clear it. I am a witness to His abounding grace and miraculous healing mercies.

> For I am persuaded that neither death nor life, nor angels nor principalities nor powers, nor things present nor things to come, nor height nor depth, nor any other created thing, shall be able to separate us from the love of God which is in Christ Jesus our Lord.
>
> —Romans 8:38–39

CHAPTER 1

IN THE BEGINNING

It was mid-May, and the air was starting to heat up as is typical in Texas. As a former professional athlete, I looked forward to regular exercise, especially weekly tennis workouts, bike riding, and my Saturday skins golf game. The only thing putting a damper on my excitement was what appeared to be the birth of a sinus infection. An upper respiratory anything is never fun, especially when spring has sprung. The days have more sunlight, and it seems as though you can get more out of each day, as long as you feel up to it.

I am a typical male patient. If I get a bad cold, I'll wait a while before I feel the need to see a doctor. As a matter of fact, I've waited months before scheduling an appointment to see a physician to resolve a condition. Usually, I'm "blowin' and goin'" all the time. As a result, I view going to the doctor as an inconvenience.

As long as I can remember, I have been driven to push on, to forge ahead, and to let nothing stop me, short of death. Where that attitude or character trait came from, I don't know for sure; but my father probably had something to do with it. Andy Manning worked hard to provide for all of us. During some holiday seasons, he took on a second job selling shoes at Sears when sales were slow with his regular job at the freight lines company.

Regardless, on the weekends, he always made time for me, usually centered around sports. We'd play pitch and catch with a baseball, shoot hoops, or he'd tell me to go long while he threw the tightest spirals with a football. He was a scratch golfer. At one time he was the number two tennis player in Memphis, Tennessee. He bowled in a league, did one-and-a-half gainers off the diving board, and narrowly missed breaking into the majors back in the day. At one point in his life, my father even drove race cars for a living. No matter what he did, Dad was committed to doing it the best he could. I never saw him *not* show up because of a sinus infection.

I guess my M.O. has been greatly influenced by my father. Specifically, I'll usually take some aspirin as an initial panacea, sort of like Windex in the movie *My Big Fat Greek Wedding*. If the condition doesn't improve, I'll find something a little stronger. If that doesn't work, then I'll break down and schedule an appointment with the doctor.

For some reason, I took a more proactive approach this time around and started using a nasal decongestant after only two weeks. A couple of weeks later, nothing had improved. At this point, I normally would have purchased a stronger over-the-counter product, but something possessed me to see my doctor, a general practitioner who had been taking care of me since I was a teenager. The day that I could get into his office, he was absent. One of his partners prescribed Keflex, a common antibiotic, to give me some relief.

One week later, nothing had changed. As a matter of fact, my condition seemed worse. I decided to call an ear, nose, and throat specialist. I hadn't seen an ENT in twenty years. He took some X-rays of my head. He told me that he noticed what appeared to be "corrosion." He asked me if I got this condition regularly. If you call once or twice a year regular, the answer was yes. He said he was going to nuke it once and for all. He wrote three prescriptions and an over-the-counter product on my walking papers.

That was Friday afternoon, June 22, 2007. I was to take all four pills once a day every morning until everything was gone. *Sweet! I should have seen this guy a long time ago because I've been experiencing crazy sinuses for years.* Anyone who has ever had a sinus infection knows what a whip it can be. I was looking forward to eradicating any future sinus conditions forever.

I began taking the meds early the following morning. I was jacked up because I was headed to pick up my good friend and golfing buddy Jeff Miles to play in our weekly Saturday skins golf game. It was a long drive to Tangle Ridge in South Dallas from where we lived in Prosper, which is on the north side. I'll never forget that round of golf because on four separate occasions, I had to take a knee as I got ready to address the ball. I suddenly felt so weak that I thought I was going to fall over. Throughout the round, I had no strength and hit the ball all over the place. Jeff knew I had started the meds and said that was probably the reason I played so poorly. Needless to say, I was exhausted. That afternoon, I napped a long time. Afterward, I felt much better.

Sunday morning, I attended church, had lunch, and took care of some real estate business later in the afternoon. Monday morning came, and as usual, I spent time reading devotional material. After breakfast, I got ready to jump in the shower. I was startled to find bruises all over my body—fifteen or sixteen of them! My first thought was, *What have the medications been doing to me?* I called the ENT right away. He told me to stop taking the prescriptions immediately and to go see my GP as soon as possible. The urgency in his voice made me feel uneasy.

On Tuesday, June 26, I got in to see my doctor. He took a lot of blood. He told me that my platelets were probably low because of all of the medications I had taken the previous three mornings. He told me to come back the next day to have more blood taken. I did, and the doctor said that my platelets had improved, but the in-depth evaluations would come back Thursday or Friday. For some reason, I knew deep down that something was seriously wrong. I told my doctor that I was a big boy and to just call me with the results. On Thursday, June 28, 2007, at 3:05 p.m., my GP called. He said, "Gregg, it looks like leukemia."

> Blessed is the man who trusts in the Lord, and whose hope is the Lord. For he shall be like a tree planted by the waters, which spreads out its roots by the river, and will not fear when heat comes; but its leaf will be green, and will not be anxious in the year of drought, nor will cease from yielding fruit.
>
> —Jeremiah 17:7–8

CHAPTER 2

MY GETHSEMANE

Have you ever been afraid? In 1972, as a sixteen year old, I think I hit three balls inside the lines while I was warming up nervously against one of the top ranked US juniors on the stadium court of the National Clay Court Tennis Championships in Louisville, Kentucky. It was my first "big time" match. In 1978, while attending SMU Dedman School of Law, I can remember being petrified standing in front of ninety-nine other students while giving a brief in a civil procedures class for forty-five minutes. In 1983, it was torture to sit through five hours of interviews for a head tennis professional position with Jack "Pop" Newell and his sons, Ken and Dave, who were also nephews of then living legend Byron Nelson.

None of those experiences holds a candle to what you feel when you hear, "It looks like leukemia." The night before His crucifixion, Jesus' anguish was so great that He sweat blood as He prayed in the garden of

Gethsemane. In an instant, I found myself standing in the middle of my own personal garden of Gethsemane. This was not one of those events in life when you simply tell yourself to suck it up and go. I had just been gut-kicked and felt sick to my stomach. I immediately gave God a call. "Please be with me" is all I said as I tried to wrap my head around what I had just heard.

I guess I could have had an anxiety attack on the spot, but I just sat on the edge of my bed for a moment and pulled myself together. Like the Bible says in Jeremiah 31:33, God really has written His Word in our hearts. How do I know? Because for some reason I thought, *It is what it is. No sense in worrying about it.* Matthew 6:27 says, "And which one of you by being anxious can add a single hour to his span of life?" (ESV).

The following day, Friday, June 29, 2007, I met with my first oncologist at one in the afternoon. "You have one of six types of acute leukemia," he said. I couldn't have just plain ole ordinary leukemia. I had *acute* leukemia. "These six types range from friendly to mean." Friendly? Excuse me, but that sounded oxymoronic. I didn't know much about cancer at that point, but leukemia, especially acute leukemia, didn't sound like it belonged in the same sentence with "friendly." He continued, "I won't know which type until we do a bone marrow biopsy." That sounded painfully invasive. How many movies have you seen with a line like that in them? I suddenly found myself living it.

To be honest, I really wasn't getting all of it at that point. As I said before, to me, going to the doctor is an inconvenience. Even though the real estate market was the softest it had been in twenty years, I was still blessed with a steady stream of clients. As a matter of fact, I planned on checking on a listing near Lake Ray Hubbard on the east side of Dallas immediately following what I thought would be just a *visit* with the oncologist. So, in my naiveté, I asked the doctor, "How long can I wait before I start any treatments? I have a lot on my platter that I need to take care of." He looked at me in total disbelief. He slid his chair closer to mine, looked me straight in the eyes, and said, "Let me put it to you this way. If you don't do anything, you have two to six weeks to live."

Wow! Ice-cold water had just been thrown in my face. In two seconds (for some reason, it only took me one second to mentally towel off) I asked, "Well then, when do we get started?" He replied, "I'm going to have a nurse take you to our lab and have your blood drawn." Lab? I had never had blood drawn in a lab before. In short order, a nurse led me down a hallway and into a large waiting room where a lot of people were sitting. I remember wondering if all of them were cancer patients. On the far side of that room, there were open double doors through which I could see six cancer patients sitting in what appeared to be recliners with IV's going into their bodies. It was a creepy scene that made me feel uneasy. We went through another doorway into a room with padded chairs, medical equipment, and computers. Absorbing the environment, I started feeling encouraged that the doctor was being pretty proactive. That feeling was short-lived. I started getting anxious because it occurred to me that the reason for his proactivity had to be the seriousness of my condition.

The attending nurse was very proficient because I hardly felt a thing when she inserted the needle into my arm. What I wasn't expecting, however, was the quantity of blood that was being taken out of me. I have had blood drawn before, but nothing like that. I asked the nurse if I could have something to eat and drink, seeing as I had no idea how long this would go on, and I didn't want to pass out. Finally, the bloodletting stopped, and I began inhaling peanut butter crackers, Reese's peanut butter cups, and soda. In the meantime, a lab technician had already begun running tests on my blood and examining the results on her computer.

As I'm eating, I'm watching her every move. Suddenly she exclaimed, "Oh my goodness!"

> Be strong and of good courage; do not be afraid, nor be dismayed, for the Lord your God is with you wherever you go.
>
> —Joshua 1:9

CHAPTER 3

REALITY SETS IN

I guess the lab tech was so focused on whatever the results were that she had forgotten that I was still in the lab. Of course, now I am startled. Who wouldn't be? I asked, "What do you mean 'oh my goodness?'"

"I'm going to get the doctor," she said and bolted out of the lab.

Within a minute, the doctor came in and said, "Gregg, we are sending you to the hospital right away."

"What for?" I asked.

"Your platelets are down to four thousand."

Still clueless, I asked, "What does that mean?"

"A normally healthy individual has anywhere between one hundred and thirty thousand and four hundred thousand platelets. With your count, any little bump or thump could trigger internal hemorrhaging. That's why you have so many bruises already. I am going to call ahead to the hospital and set you up for an infusion of platelets," the doctor replied.

Wow again! Physically, I didn't feel any different than I usually felt. Mentally, however, I was shell-shocked. Is this really happening? I just had to trust the doctor and head on over to the hospital from the oncology clinic. Just as I was about to leave, the doctor told me one more thing, and it was prophetic. He said, "Here's my cell phone number. If blood starts showing up in your urine or in your mouth, call me immediately." With that *positive* thought, I exited the clinic at three o'clock. Checking on my lake listing became a distant memory.

After I climbed into my SUV, I sat back and tried to digest everything that I had experienced over the past two hours. I picked up my cell phone and called my sweetheart, Marlaine. We had met in February 2006 in a bus transfer line in Las Vegas where Keller Williams Realty was holding its national convention. At the time, I had no idea that God would bless my life with her. Very attractive, outgoing, energetic, and friendly, Marlaine and I struck up a casual conversation and in the process discovered that we were both from the Dallas area. To make a long story short, she not only became my girlfriend, but also my best friend and confidant.

I hadn't told her about my short conversation with my GP the day before. When I told her what I had just learned and that I was driving to the hospital as soon as we finished our conversation, she broke down. I had been fine until then. But in typical male fashion, I tried to hide my emotions from her so that she would see that I was being strong in the hope that she would be strong as well.

As soon as we ended our conversation, I called my oldest sister, Teresa, who has always treated her baby brother like a second mother. She and her husband, John, were literally just returning to Fairview, Texas, on the northeast side of Dallas, from a trip. I gave her a brief synopsis of what was going on and where I was headed. She said, "We'll meet you there."

The last time I can remember driving with my hands at the ten o'clock and two o'clock position on a steering wheel was in high school driver's education. But with my platelet count at a super critical level, I was meticulously checking traffic in my side and rearview mirrors to avoid any little bump or thump like my life depended on it, which it did.

Twenty minutes later, I arrived at the hospital. I went immediately to the emergency room as instructed. Teresa and John were already there waiting for me! My prior experiences with hospital emergency rooms told me that I was probably going to be there awhile, especially on a Friday afternoon when hospital emergency rooms start to get very busy. Usually, unless you are delivered there by ambulance, you have to sign in, sit in a chair with all of the other emergency patients, and wait your turn. As I said before, I actually felt physically normal. I walked right up to the registration desk. Two nurses were at the window, one sitting and the other standing. I told the one sitting who I was. The one standing immediately took over and told me to come with her. At that point, the severity of my condition really became evident because this nurse had been *waiting* for me to arrive and took me ahead of everyone else.

I was taken to one of the emergency rooms, told to lie down, and prepped for an IV line through which I would be infused with platelets. A nurse gave me one Tylenol tablet to prevent a potential headache and one Benadryl tablet to counter any potential allergic reaction to the infusion. Already I was thinking, *Good grief! Another needle is being stuck into my arm when I just got rid of the last one!* After the process had been completed, the nurse came in and told me that my platelets were up to forty-seven thousand, and I was free to go. Right away, I praised God and simultaneously thought that I was already on my way back. This was the best news I had received in over twenty-four hours.

I felt so upbeat and relieved that I asked Teresa and John if they wanted to go to dinner. They agreed to go, and off we went to Outback Steakhouse, where I proceeded to have a steak, mashed potatoes, and a thirty-two ounce Foster's Lager to celebrate! I had no idea that would be the last substantive meal I would ingest for a long time.

I've always seen the glass half full. I am also practical and a realist. As a result, I typically hope for the best, yet plan for the worst. So the following Saturday morning, June 30, I set out to take care of as many personal items as possible so that my mind could get totally focused on dealing with one thing—cancer. I washed clothes, cleaned the house, trashed things that needed trashing, paid off bills, organized anything that appeared disheveled, and dug up my will. If necessary, I wanted to update it so that the idea of property dissemination wouldn't be a burden to anyone in my family should I die. I discovered that my ex-wife was scheduled to be the beneficiary of just about everything. It was the first time in a long time that I had thought about her and how unfortunate it was that our fifteen-year marriage ended the way it did. Nevertheless, I shook it off, proceeded to redo those necessary portions of my will, and then got it notarized.

It's amazing how good it makes you feel to take care of the smaller details in life. I felt empowered. As a matter of fact, I felt so good that I did a bit of lead generation that afternoon. That night I ate, watched a bit of TV, and hit the hay. All seemed normal in my world. That feeling evaporated on Sunday morning. I woke up with a bad taste in my mouth. I was spitting out blood. No one told me that infused platelets have a life span of forty-eight to seventy-two hours. I called the doctor immediately. He said, "Gregg, pack a bag. You're going to the hospital." Reality was setting in.

> Give ear, O Lord, to my prayer; listen to my plea for grace. In the day of my trouble I call upon You, for You answer me.
> —Psalm 86:6–7 (ESV)

CHAPTER 4

THE GOOD, THE BAD, AND THE UGLY

On Sunday morning, July 1, I found myself in a surreal drive with Marlaine as we headed toward the *first* hospital. I was tanned and, from an outward appearance, looked healthy. I certainly didn't feel poorly. But when you wake up spitting blood, you know something isn't right to say the least. I had packed a small duffle bag with my version of a survival kit: a small Bible, devotional reading material, soft athletic socks, flip-flops, underwear, warm-up suit, black T-shirt, black shorts, toiletries, golf cap, and sunglasses. You might be thinking sunglasses are odd. But I figured it was in my best interest to take them because (1) hospitals are predominantly white and I didn't want to be snow blind; (2) there was a good chance that I would be on my back for an unknown period of time, and they may just help me sleep; and (3) I would be looking at bright lights quite a bit, and they would help with any eye strain.

After I had gone through the admittance process, I was immediately taken to one of the emergency rooms again. It was determined that I needed another infusion of platelets. Another IV was inserted into one of my veins, and a young nurse gave me a Tylenol tablet. Shortly after the platelets started to course through my veins, I felt a chill. In seconds, I started to quiver. Within a minute, I began to experience uncontrollable tremors. The nurse and an emergency room doctor came in and discovered that the Benadryl tablet that should have been given to me in addition to the Tylenol had not been. Another fluid was added to the IV to counter the tremors. I had no idea that this was a warning sign of what was to come.

My doctor paid me a visit shortly after I had checked into my room. He reminded me that he wouldn't know which of the six forms of acute leukemia I had until a bone marrow biopsy was performed. I've never been afraid of needles, but I had heard stories about the size of bone marrow biopsy needles. I have to admit that the thought of being harpooned by one of them was making me a bit apprehensive. Obviously it was necessary, but I wasn't looking forward to the event.

The procedure was scheduled for seven-thirty on Monday morning, July 2. I knew it was the first step in what ultimately seemed like an endless series of steps to see if my life could be saved. I still hoped for the best but planned for the worst to help deaden the effect of bad biopsy news. Have you ever heard the expression *man up*? Have you ever told someone to *man up*? Has anyone ever told you to *man up*? Do you even know what it means to *man up*? If you do, do you know how to *man up*?

For me, *manning up* means looking up to my heavenly Father. I needed supreme help. There was no way I could handle all of this on my own. Bucking up when you twist an ankle is one thing. But facing cancer is altogether different. It was and is a life-altering proclamation. I have always recognized and acknowledged the seriousness of cancer as it pertained to others. But I never grasped or felt the gravity of it until now. You can't until you've personally experienced it. Initially, it shakes you to the core. Nevertheless, when I immediately looked up and reached up, a bit of peace entered into me. He gave me instant strength that enabled me to *man up* on the spot.

The bone marrow biopsy was conducted right on time in my room. A local injection deadened the area where the specialist stuck me with the needle. Hence, the procedure was painless, much to my surprise.

It was after the deadening had worn off that I felt the aftereffects of being stuck. I was told that the hospital lab was slammed, and since the Fourth of July holiday was on the horizon, I might not know the results until July 5! Well, I'm thinking that if I have acute leukemia, and I'm already spitting blood, time is wasting. It was bittersweet—we needed to get after this thing, but I wouldn't mind putting off knowing the results.

The rest of the day was uneventful, filled with watching TV, reading, eating, and basically acclimating myself to the hospital environment. Then, early that evening, the doctor unexpectedly returned with the results. I was prepared for the worst possible verdict. I had almost convinced myself that it didn't matter if I had the meanest kind of acute leukemia because I would begin the final journey home. Plus, I had lived a truly great life with only a few regrets for which I would like to take some mulligans.

Then the doctor smiled and told me that I had a friendly type. Without warning, I burst into tears. I didn't know until that moment what life and living meant to me. It was *good* to feel that emotion. However, as fast as that emotion leaped forward, it left just as quickly because the doctor told me that although acute promyelocytic leukemia (APML) is a friendlier disease, my condition was very serious, and we had to get busy pronto.

The next procedure was scheduled first thing the following morning, Tuesday, July 3. I was taken to one of the hospital's surgery rooms. I was given a local deadening injection, rolled onto my left side, and remained awake throughout the operation. A peripherally inserted central catheter (PICC) was surgically inserted into my jugular vein on the right side of my neck. According to my doctor, the PICC allowed chemotherapy infusion and blood extraction into and out of my body most effectively.

About an hour and a half later, I was wheeled back to my room. That whole day went on and on with medical personnel coming and going, doing this and administering that to my body, all in preparation for what I was going to have to endure. Finally, by early afternoon, I was left alone to ponder and recuperate from everything that had taken place.

By six o'clock that evening, I was physically, mentally, and emotionally exhausted. I had been lying in bed all day, and now my gown and bed linens were wet. I figured that the events of the day had stressed me out more than I expected and caused me to sweat. I thought about having the nurse come in, change my linens, and help me with a fresh gown, but I was just too tired to mess with it. I thought I would sleep until the next morning and get a fresh start with the gown and sheets, but the moist situation had become intolerable. Roughly two hours later, I couldn't stand it anymore. On top of that, I felt extremely weak.

I decided to push the call button for the nurse. I told her about my predicament, and she came in to help. She pressed the controls to automatically raise the head portion of my bed. Without warning, everything went dark. The next thing I knew, I was coming to and saw three nurses feverishly at work over my body. I was coherent enough to know this was *bad*. Suddenly, a fourth nurse burst into the room. One of the nurses exclaimed, "Thank God you're here." What had happened was that the PICC had come out of my jugular vein. I had not been sweating. I had been bleeding. When my gown and bed linens were taken away, I saw just how much I had bled. It was *ugly*. No wonder I was so weak. I am grateful that the IV specialist just happened to be on my floor. She knew exactly how to reinsert the PICC and tighten the sutures.

Two nights later, a different nurse was taking care of me on her shift. As she was putting another bag of fluid on my IV stand, she commented, "You sure gave us a scare the other night." I turned to look at her and said, "I guess by that you mean the worst could have happened to me." Without looking at me, a faint smile appeared on her face, and she gently nodded in the affirmative. Why I felt compelled to call the nurse that night is beyond me. But I am certain God had something to do with it. If I hadn't, how ironic it would have been to go Code Blue—hospital vernacular for someone needing resuscitation for cardiac arrest—before my cancer treatments even started.

> Through the Lord's mercies we are not consumed, because His compassions fail not. They are new every morning.
> —Lamentations 3:22–23

CHAPTER 5

TRANSFORMATION

Once things were back to normal, which is again oxymoronic in itself, the oncologist paid me a visit to explain what I could expect over the next three weeks. He termed it "the gauntlet." With acute anything, the treatments needed to be acute, that is, extreme.

During the first week, my body would get introduced to substances that would not incapacitate me, but they would immediately start to attack mutant cells, cells that were the result of my chromosomes 15 and 17 getting together and having a wild party. During the second week, the fluids being put into my veins would start to make me feel weaker as a result of good cells being put to death along with the bad cells. The third week would be DEFCON 1 for me—that period of time in which I would have to be strong to survive the nuclear holocaust taking place within.

In the prime of life, at the peak of physical condition, I weighed 178 pounds with a resting heart rate in the upper forties and lower fifties on average. I could skip rope over five thousand skips without a miss. It took an hour and forty-five minutes. I did it twice: once at twenty-one and again at twenty-seven. Twenty-four years later, when I was admitted into the hospital, I was still fairly fit and fortunate to be without the spare tire around the middle. Nevertheless, some muscle had converted to fat, repositioned itself around my sides and rear, and I weighed 195 pounds. At six feet tall, that isn't bad, but my personal standards told me that it could be considerably better.

As I mentioned before, with aggressive cancer comes aggressive treatments. In those first three weeks, a huge amount of alien fluids were sent via IV into my body. I could sense my body telling me that it was being bombarded. The first week didn't present anything that was disconcerting. I still got up on my own, moved around with relative ease, and went to the bathroom like a normal person.

However, during the second week, my appetite started to wane. My hair started to fall out ever so slightly, as evidenced by what I could see on my pillows. It was during this time that a nurse's aide popped into my room and, with sheers in hand, boldly proclaimed that she was there to shave my head. I asked her why even though I knew the answer. She said matter of factly that I was going to lose my hair anyway. All I can say is that the bald look works on Michael Jordan, but not on me.

That would be the last time I would consciously look in the mirror for a long time. I had seen the effects of cancer and cancer treatments on others, and I didn't want to see whatever the effects would be on me. I wanted to stay positive about myself, and seeing any gradual degradation of my physical appearance would not contribute to maintaining a healthy and strong attitude.

The third week was indeed my Armageddon. Everything inside of me was literally being put to death. I had become so weak, I could barely speak. One day one of the attending nurses came in dressed with what could be described as protective gear. She was carrying a bag of bright orange fluid. What stood out the most were the thick neoprene blue gloves that went up to her elbows. Naturally, I had one overriding question. "What's the deal with the gloves?"

She very politely responded, "I have to be careful not to get any of the chemical on my skin."

"Excuse me?" I asked. "You have to be careful not to get any of that stuff on your skin, but you're going to put it into my body?"

"This fluid helps kill everything, the good with the bad," she explained.

I tried to add a bit of levity to the situation and asked, "If you are white washing everything inside me, how is it that I still have any red blood left?"

That got a giggle out of her, and she said, "I know what you mean."

Another day during the gauntlet, my room started to go dark again. When I opened my eyes, in addition to the PICC line in my jugular, I noticed an IV in the crook of my right elbow, an IV in the back of my left hand, small oxygen tubes being placed into my nostrils, and nurses and Marlaine packing me head to toe in ice. Cold compresses were being placed and replaced repeatedly on my forehead. Ice was even tucked into my armpits. My temperature was approaching 105° F! That's pretty amazing when you consider the temperature of my room never exceeded 65° F. Fortunately, my temperature started to come down before my brain reached the baking point.

Throughout the gauntlet, I was given a steady dose of pills to counteract a variety of potential reactions and side effects from the chemotherapy, such as headaches, nausea, and abdominal pain. At one point, my stomach started cramping. The pain intensified exponentially until I had to get up so that I could get to the bathroom.

Quite frankly, I don't remember who helped me walk to the toilet. All I know is that I thanked God that I made it and that there was a handicap rail next to the can to hold onto. I gripped with all of my might because of the gut-wrenching pain. What passed out of me was, for lack of a better description, black tar. I was sweating and exhausted from what appeared to me to be death leaving my body. The perspiration was so bad that I needed a new gown.

I told the nurses what had happened. Evidently, the event raised concern because a CAT scan of my abdomen was ordered for the following day. I remembered being placed in a wheelchair and taken to radiology with my stomach still killing me. When I got there, two other patients (one on a gurney, the second also in a wheelchair) were waiting to have their pictures taken. Distress was etched on their faces. I wondered if mine looked as tormented as theirs. I honestly couldn't believe I was waiting in a pain line. The crazy thought that popped into my head was that I guess there's always room in life for stuff like this.

The male X-ray technician could sense that I was hurting and took great care in positioning me on the table. He asked me how I got the bruises on my forearms and knuckles. I hadn't even noticed them. I told him they must have happened from the intensity of choking the handicap rail during my battle on the great white porcelain throne the previous day. Fortunately, the X-rays showed that there was no blockage.

Each day when my original oncologist came into my room to check on me, he assured me that we were "right on schedule and following the plan perfectly." After a couple of weeks, he went on a vacation that had been planned before I arrived on the scene. One of his partners, a lady doctor, took over. The first day she came into my room, she gave me some shocking news. The potential cure portion of my treatments had inadvertently been left out of my therapy regimen for the previous nine days! Teresa just happened to be there. Although outwardly fairly calm, I could tell she was about to blow a gasket.

In addition to being very thorough, the pinch hitting doctor was extremely cool, calm, and collected. More importantly, she assured me that it was just a hiccup and not to be worried. Are you kidding me? Don't be worried when the potential cure hasn't been administered for nine days? What happened to "we are right on schedule and following the plan perfectly?"

A couple of days later, the lady doctor came into my room and made a mind-blowing monumental recommendation. She said that I should go to Medical City Dallas because she knew of a doctor there that specialized in leukemia and lymphoma. In effect, she was telling me without saying it that I would get better care there than where I was. Am I going to say no to a doctor that is basically telling me that my chances are better elsewhere? I don't think so. My sister was on the same page.

As a result, arrangements were made to transfer me to Medical City Dallas. At that point, I wasn't totally coherent because of all of the drugs that were flowing through my veins. But Teresa was completely in control of the situation and watched a couple of emergency medical technicians put me on a gurney, roll me out of my room, into an elevator, out of the hospital, and load me onto an ambulance. I barely remember the ride, but a funny thing happened on the way to Medical City. The head portion of my gurney collapsed in route and slammed to the floor! The EMT with me in the back of the ambulance showed some panic but remained cool about it. Due to the drugs inside my body, I didn't feel anything other than being mildly startled. In retrospect, that was probably a good thing. Ultimately, the ambulance service sent three letters to me apologizing for the incident and hoped that there weren't any complications as a result. I'm pretty sure they were trying to show good will in the hope that a legal action wouldn't be brought against them.

I was checked in and taken to what the medical personnel at Medical City affectionately refer to as Twelve South—the twelfth and highest floor of all of the buildings that make up the Medical City complex. I did not know it at the time, but it is also the floor on which the sickest of the sick are put. It was nearly the equivalent to being put into quarantine. There was a sign outside my door that read DO NOT ENTER if you are sick or if you even *think* that you *might* be sick. Anyone that came in was required to wear masks and wash their hands with antibacterial soap.

Every floor in major hospitals has an ample number of rooms on it. Twelve South is no different. What I didn't know at the time was that I had only eight floor mates, an indication of the severity of the condition of the company that shared Twelve South with me. Sadly, I know of at least three of them that are no longer with us.

My new oncologist immediately took the ball and ran with it. With a no-nonsense approach, he told me that he had a success equation in mind and that it would be implemented right away. Over twenty years ago, two Chinese doctors in research and development had discovered a potential cure for APML. My new oncologist was proceeding forward with that treatment for me. I would be remiss if I didn't say how thankful

I am for what I would call the ultimate dollar that funded their research. I now firmly believe in giving regularly to the Leukemia Society to further its advances because you never know when your dollar will become the ultimate dollar for someone else.

The first thing that was determined necessary was to surgically remove the PICC line from my neck and surgically implant a double mediport in my chest. The double mediport became my new best friend. It made it easier to infuse and extract fluids. Occasionally, I could feel a change of needles, but it beat the heck out of being stuck in the arms, hands, or wherever else a needle can be stuck.

The barrage of IV fluids continued. My weight soared to 225 pounds! I had become the proverbial beached whale. I didn't even recognize my own legs, ankles, and feet. I felt empathy for those suffering from obesity. Matthew 7:1–3 came to mind, which translated into contemporary terms says that you should take a real good look in the mirror before you make a comment about someone else. You never know what has caused them to look the way they do. To this day, that Scripture comes to mind when I see what I consider today to be an *extraordinary* person.

Another day, a nurse came into my room carrying a bag of cobalt blue liquid. It was the prettiest substance

I had seen since I had been in both hospitals. I told the nurse that I hoped it worked as beautifully as it looked. She hoped for the same and added, "This will turn your urine blue."

"Anything else?" I asked.

"In some instances, it has turned patients' corneas blue," she replied.

"Oh come on! Are you kidding me?"

"No, that's for real," she said.

Well, that stuff certainly was powerful. It not only made me pee a great deal, but it also made me feel like I was a new source of Tidy Bowl! It didn't turn the whites of my eyes blue, but being blue-eyed, I almost regret that it didn't. I think I could have had some fun with that.

My inner circle never showed concern in front of me and never, ever revealed any shock at my phone booth transformation. My doctor, however, did not hold back. He ordered sonograms to make sure clots were not forming in my lower extremities. Blood clots? I thought, *Geez, what's next?* Well, echocardiograms were next to make sure my heart was still strong enough to continue to endure the old Timex watch test that I was going through. It confirmed that I was able to "take a lickin' and keep on tickin'."

With everything that was being done to help save my life, according to the success equation, there were still contingency measures taken to protect against any potential pitfalls. The bittersweet here is that you have a tacit understanding of the potential pitfalls whether you can define them or not. Nevertheless, worry doesn't contribute to the success equation. So I asked God for help. Within the instability of the medical moment, Isaiah 33:6 says God will be the stability of our times. I had to keep my eyes on Him. In that way, the physical stretch of an additional thirty pounds in three weeks did not morph into three hundred pounds of mental angst.

God helped me with what was very uncomfortable and completely out of my control. Ultimately, the fluids in my tissues decreased. The swelling disappeared. I accidentally got a glimpse of what was left after I had taken my first shower since I had been admitted into the *first* hospital. I had little, if any, muscle definition left, especially in my legs. Tight skin was now wrinkled. A perpetually tanned body was now pasty white. My face was drawn and gaunt. I weighed 183 pounds. I had lost forty-two pounds in three weeks! At this point, I had been a hospital resident for six weeks.

I couldn't help but think how far I had fallen in such a short period of time. I was grateful that no one ever let on as to how badly I looked. To this day, I am humbled by the unflinching love Marlaine poured out for me when it would have been very easy for her to simply leave. With me from the beginning, she may have shuddered at my appearance on the inside while I was infused, transfused, injected, scanned, and so on, but she never let on. With the way I looked, there was only one way to go, and that was up. At least my eyes were clear and bright. I had begun to see life in a whole new light.

> The lamp of the body is the eye. If therefore your eye is good, your whole body will be full of light.
>
> —Matthew 6:22

CHAPTER 6

NOT IF, BUT WHEN

I had traveled down a primrose path my entire life right up until 2004. That year I experienced, six weeks apart, a couple of trips to the hospital emergency room as a result of kidney stones, one of which was so debilitating I had to be hauled off from my home in an ambulance. (I discovered the ninth wonder of the world because of those kidney stones—morphine!) In 2005, I threw my shoulder out of socket while trying to hit a kick serve in a pro-am tennis match. In 2006, I got food poisoning from eating salmon. Then, in 2007, I was told I had leukemia. The point is this: things can be going great and then turn on a dime; be grateful for every good day.

At one point during the barrage of treatments, transfusions, infusions, and blood extractions, I had an experience I'll never forget. One morning I was weaker than usual. I hadn't eaten, and I hadn't had any fluids to drink. Regardless, according to schedule,

I had to have a considerable amount of blood drawn for the regimented testing. Marlaine was in the room with me along with one nurse. I was sitting up at the time. Shortly after the nurse had extracted what she needed, I told her that I felt light-headed. Thirty seconds later, I told her that I *really* felt light-headed. In a flash, everything started getting dark again. The next thing I knew I heard the nurse barking at me to say something. As I asked her what she wanted me to say, I noticed that there stood my oncologist, his physician's assistant (PA), one of the chemo nurses, and two more EMTs with a gurney just outside the door. I thought, *Now what?*

They put me on it, hustled me into an elevator, and took me to the emergency floor of the hospital. I was coherent enough to know that I was in trouble and to pray for God to keep His hand on me. I was wheeled into the *serious* emergency room at ten forty-five in the morning. It's the largest of all of the emergency rooms located directly across from the nurses' station and outfitted with *serious* equipment. God's response? Seven different medical personnel attended to me to ensure my continued presence on earth. At one point, I was given a substance called vancomycin through another IV. In short order, I went into uncontrollable tremors accompanied by the chills for over half an hour. (I once went into full body cramps for two and a half hours on a bus ride from Wichita Falls following a three and a half hour high school tennis match; I would take that ten times over the uncontrollable tremors and chills.) Marlaine told me that seven blankets were placed on top of me to help warm me up.

To make another long story short, seven hours later, I was told that I was in the clear and that I was going to be moved to a room on another floor for observation. I discovered later that morning that all of those attending thought that I was having a heart attack! In reality, I had what's known as a vasovagal response to the blood extraction that was initiated by dehydration and a lack of nutrition. In other words, I passed out while I was sitting up. One of the male nurses came in with a clipboard to take down my medical history. I asked, "Are you serious? Don't you have all of it already?" He calmly answered that it was a matter of protocol. Somehow, I could recall most of it. As I finished the litany of things that had happened to me, I looked at him and asked, "What else could go wrong?" Without cracking a smile, he looked up from his clipboard and said, "Don't even go there."

Often, like being ambushed, our trials came out of nowhere. They are permitted by God. He is not a cruel God. Quite the opposite—He is a loving God. Nevertheless, I'm convinced that there are purposes behind these trials. First, trials prove the reality of our faith. How do you know your faith is real? By the way you react when your faith is in the fire.

Second, trials produce stability. In James we are taught to slow down, take a deep breath, and have a patient perspective when our faith is tested. Look what happened to Job. He lost everything. In Job 1:21 he said, "Naked I came from my mother's womb, and naked shall I return there. The Lord gave and the Lord has taken away; blessed be the name of the Lord." It isn't what's taken from you. It's what you do with what you have left.

Third, trials promise the crown of the life to come. My life didn't hit a speed bump; it hit the wall. Nevertheless, I was blessed after I was broken. I was crowned in the crucible of my experience. I learned to lean. I learned that I was second and to stay second. I guess the bottom line is that my cancer trial forced me to rest, to slow down, so God could heal me. The reset button for my immune system was hit by a team of incredible medical personnel, but God hit the reset button to my soul.

My brethren, count it all joy *when* you fall into various trials, knowing that the testing of your faith produces patience.

—James 1:2–3 (emphasis added)

CHAPTER 7

CAREGIVERS

There is power in disease. It can be incredibly overwhelming. But there is great power in faith, a strong medical team, medicine, and caregivers. Caregivers are the unsung heroes; the tangible support staff that provides the intangibles that can make or break the success equation for overcoming any difficult situation in life. I would liken them to the special teams in sports. They fill in the critical gaps that the doctors and nurses can't or don't have time to fill.

Whether through encouraging words, physical touch, room presence, telephone calls, or prayer, you know the caregivers are with you, keeping life as normal as possible while you are going through the daily grind of your battle. Where you lack in physical strength, their care, concern, and compassion aids in your mental toughness to march forward. Without them, I shudder to think how I could have made it.

Being in a medical jungle can be oppressive. My caregivers were so faithful to be there whenever they could, even when they really didn't have much time or after a long day at their jobs. And when they weren't there, I knew that they were steadfastly praying for me. I never thought about their stress level, what they dealt with as caregivers. To be honest, I didn't know they even had a name until I read a book written by a cancer survivor months after I had been released from the *second* hospital.

It reminds me of times when I played pressure-packed tennis matches in juniors. When I exited the court, my father would always be there offering congratulations or condolences. Occasionally, he would offer one unusual comment I didn't understand or at least fully appreciate until many years later when I became a serious tennis coach with a vested interest in my players. He would say, "I played harder than you did." You see, caregivers have a vested interest in you when there is a strong social, familial, or spousal bond.

I think, in some ways, that caregivers go through more than the patients psychologically and emotionally. What drives them? I believe God-given gifts of love and compassion. Day in and day out, caregivers have your back. Just knowing that someone cares that much to put their lives on hold so that yours can be as normal as possible while it is in the grip of cancer is humbling to say the least.

My oldest sister, Teresa, my second sister, Francine, and Marlaine were always there providing invaluable injections of emotional B_{12}. Teresa discovered what it was like to be a real estate agent in addition to being my real estate assistant. She temporarily moved out of her home and into mine. She monitored my listings, helped bring three transactions to close, brought documents to the hospital that needed my signature, kept track of my eroding personal finances, and loved my four-legged daughter Ginger as her own. (Her husband, John, was really cool about the whole thing and rediscovered what was involved in having to take care of their home and himself by himself.) In a word, Teresa was phenomenal.

Francine is a night owl. For as long as I can remember, she functions better than most after hours. In addition to being creative and artistic and an interior decorator/designer and stager of some of my listings, she has the gift of gab to say the least. That was a perfect fit for me because while the hospital was teaching me how to be an insomniac, it was rare for there to be a lack of conversation. There were many hours in which she would simply sit with me, talking about sports or life in general. It relaxed me more than she ever knew. Uncharacteristically, on a couple of occasions, the room went silent. She had somehow fallen asleep curled up under a blanket in one of the chairs in my refrigerated room. It was wonderful having Francine around on those long nights.

When many would have ejected from the whole situation, Marlaine didn't leave me. She saw me at my worst moments, some of which were gross even to me. I never saw her flinch at the sight of my blood, urine, regurgitations, tremors, sweat, odors, and the like. Whether I was being infused, transfused, or biopsied, Marlaine was rock solid. Every time I had an unexpected adventure into the emergency room, she was there. While working full time for a new home builder, a ten to seven job, she still managed to hustle over to the hospital immediately after work. There were times when she was exhausted. Regardless, she still managed to put on that beautiful smile for me. When she entered the room, she would always greet me with "hello, handsome." But she did something that was above and beyond. One night I was really struggling and losing my grip. Somehow she managed to find enough space between the lines attached to my body to lie next to me on my bed and hold me. Words cannot express how Marlaine helped me get through that night. I love her like no other.

Last but not least, I must mention one last caregiver that cannot speak English, has four legs, and sheds a lot. Ginger, my fifty-five pound golden retriever-chow mix rescue dog, and I have been together for over ten years. I kept photos of her that had been taken by Teresa on a nightstand near my bed. Anyone that is a dog lover knows the extraordinary extent of a dog's faithfulness. Teresa had not only been taking care of her but also had been speaking my name to her on a daily basis. Knowing that simple fact strengthened my resolve to make it so that I could get back to Ginger. Even though Teresa had moved into my home, there were times that I knew Ginger was all alone guarding the house and contributing her energies the best she knew how. You never know what you are going to get with a rescue dog, but Ginger is extremely bright, emotionally balanced, and loving toward everyone. I know it sounds weird, but I could sense a long-distance connection between us, and it helped drive me to get strong enough to get back to her.

> Two are better than one because they have a good return for their work; if one falls down, his friend can help him up. But pity the man who falls and has no one to help him up!
> —Ecclesiastes 4:9–10 (NIV)

CHAPTER 8

IN THE ZONE

From the beginning, I knew that I could be part of the disease or part of the cure. As a result of a lifetime of sports experience, especially competitive, nail-biting, win or lose situations, I was prepared to be part of the solution. Amazingly, I once ran a punt return back for a touchdown on the last play of a football game. I also made a half-court shot as time expired to win a basketball game. So, in the hospital, it was paramount to have a positive attitude and to always stay in the moment even if I was potentially in the last moment.

In countless tennis matches, I was presented a choice between the past, the present, and the future. Was I going to stay upset at a missed shot, disappointed that I was behind in the score, or worry that the hole I found myself in was deep and I might not climb out of it? None of the above was a viable, proactive, positive approach. I had to concentrate on the present, and play one point at a time. This would not guarantee a successful outcome, but it guaranteed the highest *probability* of a successful outcome.

How do you eat an elephant? One bite at a time. How do you climb a mountain? One hand hold and one foot hold at a time. My battle with this disease would be my most difficult match, my mammoth, my Mt. Everest. I had no idea how empowering, how uplifting, how regenerating my private moments of peace in the presence of God would be. They were like toweling off after winning an intense point or a changeover after an excruciating game to catch your breath and gather your wits. My private time, usually between two and four in the morning, helped me to recharge and psych up for the day and the impending workouts with fluid bags, needles, urinals, nausea, chills, sweats, the myriad of incessant pills, and so on.

In the movie *For Love of the Game,* Kevin Costner plays a sure-to-be hall of fame baseball pitcher for the Detroit Tigers named Billy Chapel. The story is centered around what ultimately is the last game he pitches against the New York Yankees at Yankee Stadium. With rabid Yankee fans screaming against him, and battling the knowledge that he will be traded or retired, Chapel is forced to focus like he hasn't focused in years. He encourages himself to laser his concentration before he pitches by saying, "Clear the mechanism." Chapel relies on this technique at critical junctures in the game.

As the story plays out, the forty-year-old is closing in on history—pitching a perfect game, a no hitter. Late in the game, fatigue is taking its toll. His arm and shoulder feel like rubber, and worry starts to pollute his confident attitude, like cancer in the body. Worry means "to divide the mind." Anxiety splits us in half, creating self-doubt. Rather than taking away the next moment's trouble, worry voids your strength for the moment in which you are engaged. When your strength is divided, your energy is wasted. In critical moments, you can't afford to have whatever power you possess to be diluted.

So the question is how do you prevent or stop worrying? But before I offer an answer, consider why we worry in the first place; we leave the present moment and start thinking about the moments that have passed or the ones that haven't arrived, tending only to dwell on what went wrong before could go wrong again. Our mechanism has to stay in the moment with which we are dealing.

His Word tells us in Philippians 4:6–7 that the best way to be successful is to "Be anxious for nothing, but in everything, by prayer and supplication, with thanksgiving, let your requests be made known to God; and the *peace* of God, which surpasses all understanding, will guard your hearts and minds through Christ Jesus." The bottom line is you talk to God. Then you shut up and listen. If you don't hear anything, what's popped into your head or beating inside your heart? If you suddenly think or feel something, that's probably the answer He is giving you, whether it makes sense or not.

If nothing is there, and you're still worried, do what 1 Thessalonians 5:17 says—just keep talking to God. Do you remember what God said to Moses? He said in Exodus 3:14, "I am who I am.". He didn't say, "I am who I was," or "I am who I am to be." That doesn't mean God hasn't done great things in the past or that He isn't going to do great things in the future. He simply wants us to rely on Him now. Surely, we should do everything we can possibly humanly do with the talents He has given us. But during those times when we just can't bridge the gap between where we are and where we want to go, He can.

Is your marketing stuck, are your teenagers proving why some wild animals eat their young, do your bills seem insurmountable, or are your nerves out of control when you're standing over your tee shot on the first hole? Ephesians 6:18 tells us to pray at all times and on every occasion. Stay in the moment, in the zone, so to speak, by simply being aware that God *is* there with you.

At the most critical moment for Chapel, he asks God for strength to get through the moment because he knows he can't make it on his own. He tries one more time to "clear the mechanism," but he can't. Chapel realizes he has to let go of his mechanism and just throw relying on His mechanism. God tells us in Matthew 11:28–29 to go to Him when we are burdened, and we will find rest.

Not once in my entire life had I ever thought that my flesh, my body, would fail. Now I was facing that possibility daily. It seemed unbelievable that the one thing I had relied on forever, especially as an athlete, was in jeopardy. It became so clear to me that therein was the rub. I no longer had control. I was taken to a place where I could do virtually nothing for myself. It seems as though that was the condition necessary for the Holy Spirit to go to work in me. I had to rely on God to enable me to stay in the moment, to stay in the zone.

You maintain my lot.

—Psalm 16:5

The Lord is my rock and my fortress and my deliverer; my God, my strength, in whom I will trust.

—Psalm 18:2

My flesh and my heart may fail, but God is the strength of my heart and my portion forever.

—Psalm 73.26

My heart and my flesh cry out for the living God.

—Psalm 84:2

CHAPTER 9

COME TO ME

The Lord says, "Come to Me, all you who labor and are heavy laden and I will give you rest" (Matt. 11:28). This verse, in the historical sense, was for the people back in the day that were suppressed by the scribes and Pharisees via their legalistic approach to religion. Jesus offered a way out from being held captive underneath this burden. However, for me personally, it is a verse that allowed me to rally from minimum physical rest and maximum mental strain.

I never slept in the normal sense, I catnapped sparingly. How could I sleep normally? So many medical personnel were charged with keeping me alive, regularly coming in and out my room around the clock, so that extended periods of sleep were impossible. I am not complaining. But sleep deprivation was the norm. If you have ever been deprived of sleep, you understand the fringe deficit— poor mental acuity.

Here's the good part. When I went to God in prayer, my heart rate slowed and my mind relaxed. I could prove it to you if I allowed myself to be hooked up to a heart monitor, but I don't want to go down that road again anytime soon. I literally could see the difference when a nurse came in to check my vitals after I had been spending time with the Lord. In addition, I was at peace, and it was easier to deal with the next round of whatever was going to be done to me.

My faith began to soar no matter how bed bound my body became. As a child, I had a recurring dream in which my bed, with me in it, would fly out of the window high above the street and the rooftops of my neighborhood below. It felt so effortless, so smooth. I was completely secure in the knowledge that I would return safe and sound. My experience in the wee hours of the morning was a recurring one, but it was no dream. The height to which the Holy Spirit was taking me above my stormy reality was calming and peaceful. Psalm 55:6 says, "Oh that I had wings like a dove! I would fly away and be at rest." The Holy Spirit became my wings, lifting me above my circumstance and providing relief from the stress.

In times of adversity, we stay closer to God through an abundance of prayer. We develop a consistent focus spending more time communing with Him. As I have stated before, God's Word says to pray without ceasing in 1 Thessalonians 5:17, to always be prayerful in Romans 12:12, and to pray at all times and on every occasion in Ephesians 6:18.

That may sound difficult and burdensome unless you think of developing the habit of continual awareness. That's what happens during adversity—we have the capacity to block things out when we need God in emergencies. However, we need to see the importance, the urgency, the necessity of God in all things, and then we'll develop the habit of continual awareness, hence continual prayer.

It is amazing how the minutes passed into hours and the hours passed into days and the days into months because He kept me through my prayers. He kept me peacefully in the now. Philippians 4:7 says that the peace of God surpasses all of our understanding and will guard our hearts and minds. I needed strength in each individual moment just to get to the next. Prayer doesn't get you around trouble; it gets you through it. If you are in the middle of the griddle, stressed out to the max, physically exhausted, up to your ears in alligators, look for a private moment in a solitary place, and go to Him.

Many are the afflictions of the righteous,
but the Lord delivers him out of them all.

—Psalm 34:19

Come to Me, all you who labor and are
heavy laden, and I will give you rest.
Take my yoke upon you and learn from
Me, for I am gentle and lowly in heart,
and you will find rest for your souls. For
My yoke is easy and My burden is light.

—Matthew 11:28–30

CHAPTER 10

THE MYSTERY MAN

There were some long nights, really long nights, at the hospital. That was due in part to the drugs and in part to the medical team members checking on me around the clock. However, two to four o'clock in the morning was typically a time of incredible silence. The only thing regularly audible was the sound of the hospital. I don't know if it was a generator or what, but whatever it was, there was a distinct rhythm to it. Sometimes it was soothing. Other times, it kept me from getting any shut-eye. It was during one of those early morning hours that the sound kept me from reading or praying. I got this insane idea to get up and go to my window. I hadn't done this without help since I had been admitted to Medical City. But I wanted to get a closer look at the night. Something was telling me that I needed to.

This was going to take considerable methodical effort and concentration. I knew what I had to do because it had been explained to me before. I first had to locate the device that controls the bed and pressed a button that raised my head. I then pulled and pushed myself to the side, careful not to get tangled up in my IV lines, sat up for a minute with my legs dangling over the edge to make sure that I wasn't going to pass out, slid my feet into my flip-flops, asked God to support me, and stood up. I felt like a newborn fawn, wobbly and unsure.

Carefully, I unplugged the vitals box, draped the cord over the shepherd's hook that extended up from the IV stand, took my "meals on wheels" and shuffled ever so slowly over to the window. When you are healthy, it is easy to take walking on your own for granted. I felt proud for the first time in a long time because I had actually accomplished something totally on my own. As I stood there, I absorbed the colors of the buildings nearby—the red letters on the side of one, the white highlights of a second, and a royal blue light strip wrapped around the top of a third. I whispered, "How American."

I was amazed at how the night felt looking out from the top of Twelve South. Traffic on LBJ Freeway in the distance was sparse, but indicated life. What are people doing at two o'clock in the morning in the middle of the week? It then hit me that I didn't even know if it was the middle of the week. Come to think of it, I don't recall ever keeping track of what day of the week it was.

As I was taking in the surroundings, I happened to look at the shorter buildings adjacent to mine that make up Medical City. About four floors beneath me, in the closest building, I noticed a room with a light on and the blinds open. There was a patient reading in bed. I could tell the patient was male, but I couldn't see his face. My only thought was, *He can't sleep either.* I don't know why I couldn't sleep more than thirty minutes at a time. But I learned to make use of it by reading, praying, listening to the hospital, or watching a little TV.

A couple of nights later, around two o'clock again, the colorful lights beckoned me to my window. I psyched up to get myself out of bed. Again, I meticulously went through the precarious routine of getting out of bed and over to the window. The experience was equally as gratifying as the time before. Just as I was about to return to my bed, I happened to glance down and noticed the same male patient was awake and reading. I felt a smile form on my face and thought that at least I wasn't the only one who couldn't sleep.

I didn't go to the window every night. I wish I could have, but many times I was too gassed to get up. However, those nights I was able to make it, the mystery man was always awake. For some reason, that seemed to empower me. I took comfort in the fact that I wasn't alone in my infirmed plight. God was using the mystery man to minister to me. It wasn't important for me to know who this man was. What was important was that God was telling me, "You're not alone," and He was with me.

In addition, I discovered that every dark night was the front door through which a new experience and a new day were waiting to emerge. Frankly, there is a treasure in every moment. Sometimes it jumps out at you. Other times it comes quietly, peacefully. But they are all around us. How odd that the dark became a source of light, a place of security, and a time of spiritual growth.

> I will give you the treasures of darkness and hidden wealth of secret places.
> —Isaiah 45:3

> Indeed, the darkness shall not hide from You, but the night shines as the day; the darkness and the light are both alike to You.
> —Psalm 139:12

CHAPTER 11

THE FOUR C'S

I made an effort to greet everyone that came into my room, especially those responsible for cleaning it and those responsible for delivering my meals. Now there were those I never got to see, but I spoke with over the phone—the folks that took my food order for each meal. In an odd sort of way, they were like the mystery man, but better. They had no faces, but at least they had voices that were always kind and familiar.

To them, I could have been just one of hundreds of faceless patients demanding another phone-ordered meal. At least I understood that. But I didn't want to be treated like that. The Golden Rule says, "Do unto others as you would have them do unto you." So I made sure that I greeted the food and beverage department people cordially. I also feel that *courteous conduct confirms Christ.* I knew that I could be a witness for the Lord by showing appreciation for what the food and beverage staff was doing for me even if I didn't feel well.

Although I was incarcerated, the faceless voice taking my order over the phone was not. It was as though she was a link to the outside. Giving her my meal order was as close to sitting in a booth at a restaurant as I could get—an experience we often take for granted. It made me feel normal. Better yet, it made me feel grateful. Colossians 4:6 (ESV) says, "Let your speech always be gracious." I made sure it was whether face-to-face or not. The person taking my order was part of my room, albeit for just a minute or two.

Frances Manning had a lot to do with the way I tried to behave during my hospital tenure. Born and raised in a pinhead-size community known as Amory, Mississippi, my mother was a dyed-in-the-wool, true blue Southern lady with a drawl to match. Expressions like "I'll swanny" and "snot rag" were the norm for her. But what was above average, way above average, was the way she treated everyone. One of the most powerful memories I hold onto to this day is how, as a little boy, my mother would lean over and tickle me with her hair as I reached up to touch her face while lying in her lap.

Many years later, I was sitting on a coffee table very close to her as she lay on a couch in our den slowly slipping out of this world and into the next as a result of cancer. I leaned over to listen to her speak softly in that amazing Southern accent. She reached up to touch my face and *asked me how I was doing*! In that moment, life seemed to come full circle from that childhood memory. She was always that way, so outwardly focused, so focused on others. She always cared so much about everyone else. I thank God that He blessed me with such a loving mother. She doesn't know it, but she helped me take my focus off of my condition and place it on all of those involved in my care.

I must admit that the medical staff inspired my attitude because they brought their best, day in and day out, to those of us that were at our worst in terms of our health. In Twelve South—residence of the sickest of the sick—I saw more Christ-like behavior than any other place in my life. Three nurses that took care of me were cancer patients themselves—not survivors, patients! Matthew 25:40 (ESV) says, "Truly I say to you, as you did it to one of the least of these, my brothers, you did it to me." It may be their job, a paid-for duty, but in my experience they performed their duty with an abundance of compassion. Christ was at work amid the ill in Twelve South. If you wanted to see God, He was there working His magic between the broken patients and the brave-hearted professionals.

As further proof, I learned of another patient on Twelve South while I was there. Her stay continued long after mine was over. Her husband and Marlaine became friends during their extended vigils. Marlaine told me that this lady was a believer, loving, courteous, and inspirational to all of the medical staff charged with her care, and perpetually upbeat all the way to the end. A memorial service was held for her in the hospital chapel, to which Marlaine and I were invited, a couple of months after I had been released. The pastor summed up what this woman brought to life—a genuine and infectious optimism and compassion for those around her. Most, if not all, of the medical staff that had taken care of her and me were in attendance. Some of the staff was visibly shaken by her departure. She had added joy to their lives. It must be so difficult for medical personnel to give so much in the hopes of seeing a restored life only to see that life expire.

The pastor asked if any of them had anything that they wanted to share. Each who did expressed how she was so positive, always smiling, and a gentle soul. For some reason, the pastor zeroed in on me. He knew that I had been a resident in Twelve South at the same time with her. He wanted me to share something, anything, with those in attendance. Again, Matthew 25:40 came to mind. I told them that they should be proud of their day-in and day-out efforts. Unfortunately, they would certainly lose patients in the future. However, all they had to do to stay encouraged was look at me and know that my life, my living, was a result of those same efforts that they gave so devotedly to my floormate.

God can take our adversity—a heart attack, an automobile accident, violent crime, bankruptcy, a marriage crisis, the loss of a loved one, cancer—and transform that pain into encouragement for the people around us. We come out of those experiences stronger and better able to comfort others. God in His grace can bring blessing out of our adversity.

> You shall love your neighbor as yourself.
> —Matthew 22:39

CHAPTER 12

FORCED FASTING

When was the last time you had a breakthrough? Perhaps you need one right now with your career, your spouse, your finances, or your health. What are some of the things you have tried to implement? More hours on the job, a weekend getaway without the kids, lottery tickets, a home gym? All of these things could work, but in your pursuit of the breakthrough, did you become obsessed with *making* things happen? A type A person (i.e., control freak) knows what I'm talking about.

I have another suggestion: seek God for the answers, the solutions, the breakthroughs. How? Develop a laser focus on Him. If you feel that you don't have the time because of the number of hours not left in the day, grab an hour or two from your sleep time, your break time, your meal time, your weekend time, and make it God's time. When you set aside a period of time for

God to work His magic within you, you will begin to experience a clarity like never before.

In my case, I had no choice but to be in a bed and take it like a man … laying down. In addition to the gauntlet of treatments I had to pass through, I was placed on a special neutropenic diet. If you have lower than normal white blood cells, you have to eat foods in which bacteria and other microscopic creatures have been put to death. I remained on this diet for quite some time until I could start eating regular food. It was, for all intents and purposes, forced fasting.

I had never fasted before. I think it's humorous when I hear people talk about giving up something like chocolate for lent. I hate to burst their bubbles, but that's not fasting. (I should mention that I was given small triangular pieces of sponge attached to plastic Tootsie Pop sticks and a mint-smelling liquid. This became my mandatory method of dental hygiene to take care of the remnants of the wonderful diet I was on. Using a regular toothbrush ran the risk of pricking a gum open and could cause me to bleed to death!) With the thought of eating normally out of the way, my concentration on my faith relationship started powering up automatically.

I know of a story where one guy needed answers to help get his country out of seventy years of captivity. He reprioritized his life, put God first, fasted, chose to concentrate religiously on listening to God for answers and, *voila*, he got them. How about another guy who fasted for forty days and nights in a desert, lasering His focus on God to overcome temptations of power, wealth, and fame? You can read about these two guys in the Bible. Daniel was the first guy, and Jesus was the second. If there was a Hall of Fame for fasting, they would be members of the original inductee class. During my forced fasting, I lost my hair, my strength, my stamina, my muscle definition, my sleep, my appetite, and my income. But I racked up a lot of one on one time with *the guy*.

When was the last time you had a truly meaningful dialogue with someone? I'm not talking about a hot sports opinion. I'm talking about a soul-searching, house-cleaning, mind-stretching conversation, especially with God? Fasting allows you to do that, if you choose. I would strongly suggest that you don't wait until some cataclysmic event disrupts your life and forces you into that mode. Take just a little bit of time to let Him speak to you in private. With practice, you'll discover that He can turn your mind-boggling conundrums into logistical midgets. Whatever He tells you, simply obey. If you don't hear something right away, just be patient, and wait until you do.

> Rest in the Lord, and wait patiently for Him.
>
> —Psalm 37:7

CHAPTER 13

HE'S UP!

My room at the hospital had become my world. There wasn't a lot I could do there, nor was there a lot I was capable of doing. To recap, I entered the hospital weighing 195 pounds. At six feet tall and fifty-one years of age, that was decent. If you recall, my weight soared to 225 pounds as a result of all of the stuff that was put into me. But now I weighed 183 with total muscle atrophy. My spirit was strong, but my body was frail and extremely weak.

Whenever I needed to get up to use one of my four urinals or shuffle to the bathroom or get to my beloved window, it took methodical effort to accomplish the objective. As much as I could or felt capable of, I would make myself get up and shuffle a few steps in my room. Depending on the time of day, severity of chemo treatments, or amount of rest I had gotten, I would push myself to go another step.

At some point, I was given a handheld portable breathing apparatus called a spirometer. I was told what the ultimate goal was. The device was designed to measure the strength of my exhaling—not only its force, but also the length of time I could maintain that force. From the get-go, the exercise showed how far I had descended. No wonder I was so gassed after just meagerly shuffling around the room. It wasn't just my legs that were weak. My lung power was virtually nonexistent. I made up my mind that I wasn't going to just practice this respiratory exercise. I decided that I was going to make it a *workout*. Otherwise, I would continue to feel, act, and look like a very unhealthy old man for Lord knows how long.

I pushed myself, drawing on the discipline from my younger athletic days. Within a week, I noticed a significant difference. My lung power started to increase. Instead of ten shuffling steps, I lasted twenty! The more I practiced, the more I shuffled, and then I started taking steps. Ultimately, I decided it was time for me to get out of my room and walk. I told the nurses what I was going to do. I wasn't sure when, but when I did I wanted them to keep an eye on me in case I cratered!

When the day came, I prayed that God would keep His hand on me no matter how far or how short the walk. Even opening the door to my room was a new process I had to calculate. I had to keep my balance and keep the IV lines clear while opening it, maneuver my "meals on wheels" so that I could get out, and make sure the heavy door didn't hit me in the rump on the way out.

Once outside, I took a moment to gather my bearings and thank God that I was out of my cell. It had been so long since I had been outside of my room standing on my own two feet instead of in a wheelchair or lying on a gurney. But now was the moment of truth. How far could I go? Could I keep my balance? Would I pass out?

Twelve South is built in a square. To a healthy individual, this would be a boring no-brainer. To me, it was a blessing. On top of that, the floors are vinyl. That meant no carpet to trip over or on which to get my wheels hung up. Off I went. Never had I been so focused on the concept of one foot in front of the other as I was that day.

Fortunately, the first part of my walk took me directly past the nurses' station. Three nurses were busy at work. One looked at me and exclaimed, "He's up!" That simple statement told me a great deal. One, I had been in bed a long time. Two, medical personnel had probably wondered if I would ever be vertical like this again. Three, now that I was, how long would I last?

As I made it past their station, I could sense three sets of eyes paying close attention. They were probably joyful but holding their collective breaths as well. I made my first left turn down the second corridor, paying attention only to what was directly in front of me. I came to a set of double doors, which would require more multitasking. Fortunately, they were relatively easy to open and slow to close. Without stopping, I came to the next left turn and continued down the third corridor. I could feel my heart pounding, and my breathing was labored. I came to a small secondary nurses' station that was unmanned. I had to stop. I hadn't felt like that since Martina Navratilova made me do suicide drills with her after one of our tennis workouts back in the eighties.

Although I was exhausted, I was overcome by an incredible wave of emotion. I wept almost uncontrollably. They were tears of joy as I thought about footprints in the sand and how God had just given me the strength to take those baby steps. For once, I was glad that no medical personnel was in sight because it was such a special private moment that I shared with Him. At that very instant, I could sense God holding me up and, in a way only He can, He let me know for the first time since I had been admitted into the first hospital that I was going to make it. No one was around. It was just me and God in a remarkably peaceful yet powerfully defining moment.

It took a couple of minutes, but I gathered my composure, psyched up, and resumed putting one foot in front of the other. I made it to the end of the third corridor, turned left one more time, and headed for *home*. Once I reached the door to my room, I had to run through my checklist of things to do to get the door open, maneuver through the opening safely, and prepare for landing. I was dragging to be sure, but I took great satisfaction in the achievement.

I had traveled through some very difficult moments, but I never gave in to hopelessness. He reached down, took hold of me, and drew me out of some very deep waters, just like Psalm 18:16 says. I had found renewed confidence and strength in my exhaustion. The following day, I made up my mind to make the journey without stopping. Each day, I upped the ante; first, to make the trip twice in one day, then three times in a day, then twice around in one trip, then twice around twice in a day until I made it five and six times in one trip without stopping. The Lord had carried me through a gauntlet. He had extended His healing mercies. Now, it was my turn to take the ball and do something special with it. I will make good use of the deliverance.

> For You have delivered my soul from death, yes, my feet from stumbling; I will walk before God in the light of life.
>
> —Psalm 56:13 (ESV)

CHAPTER 14

JEHOVAH JIREH

Near the end of 2007, my doctor pronounced me well enough to leave the hospital. It had been a six-month journey. He said that I could become a functioning member of society again. That meant I could actually go outside and circulate among the active without a mask. Teresa came to pick me up, and we coordinated when she would get to the porte-cochère of the building's lobby so that I could minimize the waiting for the car.

I put on my shorts, T-shirt, flip-flops, golf cap, and sunglasses. Placed in another wheelchair, I exited my room with medical personnel wishing me well. I took the ride twelve floors down on the elevator to the ground floor. I had no idea that I would soon experience another flood of emotion. The nurse's aide pushed me through a maze of corridors until I reached the lobby in which I could see when Teresa pulled up. A moment later, there she was. I was pushed through the automatic lobby doors and right up to the car. I slowly got up, slid in, and closed the door. We sat there for only a second as I soaked in the freedom. Man, it felt good to be out of the hospital. But the moment she started to pull away, I was blindsided by an unexpected feeling—fear.

In the movie *Shawshank Redemption*, James Whitmore and Morgan Freeman play inmates that are eventually paroled. They were institutional men; that is, they had been in prison so long that prison had become their home, their security blanket. Whitmore's character was overwhelmed by the uncertainty that lay ahead and chose to take his life at the halfway house. Freeman decided that he could either get busy living or get busy dying. I now have a better appreciation and understanding of their initial fears. As we drove away, I felt relief but insecurity because I was leaving the very environment that had kept me alive. I was now going to have to gradually take a greater role in the responsibility for furthering that goal.

On the drive back to my home in Prosper, the first thing that I noticed was how beautiful the day was with blue skies and a spattering of clouds. I couldn't help but think how awesome it was to be in traffic and seeing people go about their lives while absorbing everything around us—a plane flying overhead, birds sitting on guide wires, a couple of people getting on a DART bus.

Thirty minutes later, we entered my neighborhood. Willow Ridge looked beautiful. There is a wonderful pond at the entrance that happened to be filled with mallards and geese. It is a pleasant tree-lined drive that meanders to a second pond in the center of the community with cascading waterfalls and a pool that my house overlooks. As we approached my home, I could see Ginger, on cue, waiting at the door. When she saw me, she started whining. I was very weak, and I knew she was going to jump up on me, but I couldn't wait to hold her. As soon as I opened the door, she was all over me. I immediately sat down so that I wouldn't fall over. She was so excited that she knocked off my golf cap, exposing my bald head. She was quivering and couldn't stop sniffing it, as if to say, "I know it's you, but where's your hair? What happened to you? Why have you been gone so long?" Tears started flowing again. Ultimately, we both settled down as I held onto her the rest of the day. She slept in my bed with me that night.

The next morning, a new reality set in. As far as my work life was concerned, I didn't know where to start. My normal routine before my illness included previewing completed new homes on the market all over the Metroplex. On average, I would spend ten hours a week looking at new products so that I would have a working knowledge of the latest and greatest in all price ranges. Now, there was no normal. I had to develop a new routine because my doctor told me to stay away from dust for a while, something that is prevalent around new-home construction.

For some reason, my mind is like a steel trap when it comes to retaining information about homes that I have seen. Whenever someone in my pipeline of leads would request my services to assist them in their search for that perfect four bedroom, three bath, three-car garage home in a certain area, usually three or four possibilities meeting that criteria would pop up in my head. Now there were some problems, big problems. First, I had no pipeline of leads, having been out of circulation for six months. Second, I had no money with which to market my services due to the exorbitant medical costs that had gobbled up my funds. Third, having been out of circulation, I didn't have a clue as to what products were available even if I had a lead.

I turned to the One, the only one who could help, Jehovah Jireh, which in Hebrew means "God is my provider." As I had so often in my hospital room, I began to pray for God's help. I didn't even know if real estate was God's will for me. Heck, I even toyed with the idea of getting back into teaching tennis. That idea quickly faded considering how I was being placed on a new two-year outpatient chemo pill therapy regimen that would make me highly susceptible to skin cancer. I had to put sunblock on just to drive my SUV, and I held an umbrella over my head when I walked to my mailbox to retrieve the mail!

I had decent medical insurance, but since I had always been healthy and stayed fit, I carried very high deductibles to keep my monthly premiums low. Using the 80/20 rule, 80 percent of the medical expenses were covered by my insurance. You might be thinking pretty good, right? It's not so good after you calculate 20 percent of a gazillion dollars as my debt that I would be paying off for years to come. The bottom line was that my once flush bank account had been flushed.

I sat down at my desk to go over all of the insurance claim receipts that had been mailed to me. I wanted to understand the costs. The first three weeks of the first hospital that I was in totaled over two hundred thousand dollars, and that didn't include the special stuff. Each chemo session was ninety thousand dollars. The cure pills alone cost seventy-five hundred dollars for a fifteen-day supply of ten pills a day. Some days I was taking twenty-five pills of assorted flavors. I don't even want to go into the astronomical emergency room costs. My mind was so boggled by the initial numbers and the stack of unopened claims that I ceased tallying everything on an Excel spreadsheet.

My prayer time was first and foremost about praising and thanking God that I was still here, that He had extended His healing mercies to me. Second, I asked Him to never let me forget the mile I had just walked. Third, no matter what His will was for me and my business, I would always love Him. Fourth, I would be an opportunistic witness, whether individually or corporately, on behalf of His kingdom and His goodness. Fifth, I would pay it forward wherever possible. Sixth, I would have a pure heart for caring for those that were seriously ill, especially those that I came across with cancer. And seventh, I would rebuild my body because He kept it from being turned to dust by this disease.

Seven real estate transactions came out of nowhere! Those seven transactions carried me through all of 2008. To this day, I go back over the numbers of that year and don't understand how they got me through. Every time I think about it, I think of the story of how the Lord fed all of those people with so few fish and even had leftovers! Praise God that He makes possible the seemingly impossible. How incredible and how enlightening that seven transactions dropped into my lap. I thought back on my emergency room encounter in which seven medical personnel, seven blankets, and seven hours highlighted the experience. If seven isn't God's number, it has to be one of His favorites, as it is used over five hundred times in the Bible.

> But Jesus looked at them and said, "With man this is impossible, but with God all things are possible.
>
> —Matthew 19:26

CHAPTER 15

Small Talk

I've always been driven, task-minded, disciplined, and unwavering toward goals. There was a time when I was obsessive to the point where I couldn't see the forest because of one tree. Don't get me wrong. Having that laser focus on your projects, your missions, and your endeavors is a good thing, provided you don't lose sight of the big picture.

Regardless, as Rick Warren puts it in his book *The Purpose Driven Life*, "It's not about you." Often when you achieve goals you feel proud, sometimes to the point of arrogance, and sometimes to the point of relief. But the best feeling is when you feel God's approval. Usually, it comes through a measure of humility. A life-altering event produces involuntary humility. It is much better if you get it voluntarily. James 4:10 (NIV) says, "Humble yourselves before the Lord, and He will lift you up."

Dedication, discipline, drive, desire, and determination—I have lived my life by them. But those full-time attributes had always been used toward the duty, the job, and the project until mortality reality set in. It's never been about perfection for me; it's always been about excellence—getting the very best out of myself. I've always enjoyed that pursuit, sometimes to the point of exhaustion and even obsession relative to my self-imposed standards.

With age and divine intervention, I was made aware of how this drive can lead to pride and being self-centered. God has since enlightened me and curbed this liability into a gift to further His kingdom command. As a result, this chronic mental cancer has been replaced with an inner peace and satisfaction that I have never known in a spirit-filled sense.

I must admit that achievement still feels good. However, a new righteous pride has now replaced the old earthly kind when I do something that from the beginning was God-centered. Frankly, I no longer pat myself on the back. Instead, what I long to hear is for God to say, "Well done, good and faithful servant."

It is amazing the influence each of us can have, one person at a time, in a world of billions, just because we ask Him to take our lives and make them a ministry. You just have to ask Him, and He will do it. The deadly cancer in my blood pointed to the deadly cancer in my mind and heart. Praise God that both are in remission!

I can't stress prayer enough. It is a gift free to you and me. It costs only a bit of your time. When you pray, you commune with God and meditate upon the fractures or leaks of mind, body, or soul in your life or someone else's. Getting real with God is not about using eloquent words or saying things that don't apply. It is simply small talk, direct talk with the all-knowing, the all-powerful, the all-loving Creator. He knows what's needed before you ask Him, but you still have to ask. Why? He wants you to humble yourself before Him by being dependent on Him.

Pride will bring any man down, yet humility will raise him up. All of us must endure various trials. However, when you are faced with a catastrophic event, when suddenly the reality of death is staring you in the face, you will get real with your small talk with God because you may be rehearsing for eternity. The revelation of mortality makes us come clean. Whatever time His grace extends to you, be a living sacrifice. Give up pride, give up yourself, and listen to Him. Declare God's glory every day even when the day isn't glorious. Be conscious of His presence, and you will be continuously connected to Him.

And when you pray, you shall not be like the hypocrites. For they love to pray standing in the synagogues and on the corners of the streets, that they may be seen by men. Assuredly, I say to you, they have their reward. But you, when you pray, go into your room, and when you have shut your door, pray to your Father who is in the secret place; and your Father who sees in secret will reward you openly. And when you pray, do not use vain repetitions as the heathen do. For they think that they will be heard for their many words. Therefore, do not be like them. For your Father knows the things you have need of before you ask Him. In this manner, therefore, pray: Our Father in heaven, hallowed be Your name. Your kingdom come, Your will be done on earth as it is in heaven. Give us this day our daily bread, and forgive us our trespasses as we forgive those who trespass against us. And lead us not into temptation, but deliver us from evil, for Yours is the kingdom, the power and the glory forever. Amen.

—Matthew 6:5–13

CHAPTER 16

FACTS OF LIFE

You may be in the middle of your own struggle. You may be asking yourself, *Why was I put here anyway? What's the use?* Something could be robbing you of your joy. Fill in this blank: I will be happy when____
_____.

When you're promoted? When you find the right person? When you get rid of the wrong person? When your bank account is flush? When you are healthy? When you are healed? Now with your answer firmly in mind, answer this: If your dream never comes true, if your ship never comes in, if your situation never changes, can you still be happy?

If not, then you need to know what you have in the Savior, the shepherd, the Christ, the Holy Spirit that dwells within or at least wants to. We have a marvelous God who listens to us, hears us, loves us, and extends His grace to us for every heartache, overdrawn account, dead-end job, failed relationship, and life-threatening illness. Because He is the ultimate lifesaver, you have everything you need. You just have to let Him in if He isn't there already. And if He is, and you haven't heard Him speak to you in a while, find a quiet place, say nothing, and listen because He knows what's on your mind and in your heart. Sometimes it's a tiny voice, sometimes a thought, sometimes an emotion stirred that signifies His presence in your life. He wants you to stop just long enough to connect.

If you are accustomed to going through life with your hair on fire, initially you'll have to force yourself to take a time-out. That takes discipline, the same discipline it takes to keep going through life with your hair on fire. But that discipline to take a bit of time to spend quietly waiting for conversation with Him will turn into desire. Eventually you will want, dare I say need, to converse with Him every day. Because no matter how much you are bruised or beaten down by the daily goings-on, His grace is sufficient, and that will give you a joy that transcends whatever can be thrown at you.

I didn't pick this fight. It picked me. Sometimes that's just the way it goes. But God is showing others through my experience how strong He is. Through me, He is showing how good He is as well. Through my weakness, He shows how strong and mighty He is.

All I could do was pray: "Lord Jesus, would you help me? I need you. You're my God. You're on the throne. You are my Rock, my refuge, my stronghold. If things don't work out, I'll still love you."

Our actions will always follow our beliefs. If you can't get out, if you can't get up, if you can't walk, you can't just pout about it. If you accept defeat, then that's exactly what you'll get. I have never been a fence-sitter. I had to decide what side I wanted to be on, the good side or the bad side of cancer, and stay on it. Until He decided to move me, I was to grow right where I was planted in that hospital room. Ultimately, He opened a door that no disease can shut.

God puts us here to honor Him. My disease was and is a way to do that. I knew I should give Him my best, win or lose, life or death. I want to talk about what He did for me, about the gift, the second chance. I honor Him with my actions and my attitude. What are you living for? What are you giving back to Him? I resolve to give Him everything I have. I leave the results up to Him. Whatever happens, He gets the glory.

In the Bible, the *inerrant* Word of God, He says 365 times "do not fear." That's a one-a-day vitamin. You must trust Him, and you need to thank Him. Nothing is impossible if you believe in Him. I waited until God let me know it was time to get up and walk. I have a platform, a strong platform, from which to witness. I honor God by utilizing the testimonial authority He has given me, and I'm just another ordinary man. A lot of people get so set in their ways. They're afraid of change. They're afraid of being stretched. I just hope that if you are one of those that resist Him, you realize how much He loves you anyway.

I'm human and make errors and omissions. But in the eternal scheme of things, I will never be lost. You don't have to follow Christ or accept Him. But if you do, I promise you this—you'll never be the same!

In the Keller Williams Realty culture we talk about "aha's" and share them with our *family members*. Just before I was to be released from the second hospital, one of my office managers called me. Toward the end of our conversation, he asked me if I had gotten any "aha's" from this experience. I told him that I had—I will never let life get in the way of life again. All around us, life is full of miracles. To experience them is simply a matter of manning up.

> Trust in the Lord with all your heart, and
> lean not on your own understanding; in
> all your ways acknowledge Him and He
> shall direct your paths.
>
> —Proverbs 3:5–6

Epilogue

On October 3, 2011, I went into the hospital for a scheduled six-month visit so that the regimented molecular testing of my blood could be done. My port had long been surgically removed, so my blood was extracted the old-fashioned way from a vein in the crook of my left arm because it had the best vein candidate. That, in itself, was odd to me considering how my *right* arm once had great veins from all of the tennis that I use to play. Now they couldn't find a good one without using a butterfly needle (a very small needle used with children) because of all of the venous scar tissue.

Once the results came in, my oncologist instead of his PA visited with me for the first time in over two years. At first, I was a bit concerned. But he put me totally at ease when he said that the results looked great, and I needed only one more visit to the hospital in about another six months.

On March 5, 2012, I made what I hoped would be my last trip to Medical City. Again, the Dracula procedure was administered to my left arm. An hour later, I saw the PA this time. She said my numbers were beautiful, and I didn't need to come back anymore! She gave me a hug. It was a private emotional moment. She advised me to have a routine complete blood count (CBC) performed by my GP once a year and added that anyone my age should have that done. If you recall, the day that I was diagnosed I was told that I had a platelet count of four thousand. On any given day, a normally healthy person has between one hundred and thirty thousand and four hundred thousand platelets streaming through the blood. My platelet count is now well over two hundred thousand.

The cancer speck in my rearview mirror is gone. There are new challenges ahead. Although my body, according to the oncologist, has aged an additional five to seven years as a result of what I went through, I take it in stride. There are more lines in my face, but more smiles. There is less muscle in my body, but more strength. There is less doubt in my mind and so much more faith.

I know that it's an understatement, but any form of cancer is a serious business. Never take life for granted. Another kindred spirit that I met in the hospital was doing well when we last spoke face to face. Six months later, I found out that she has gone on to heaven. I am so grateful for God's grace.

I guess the point of all of this is that when you are faced with a cataclysmic, life-altering event, don't ever give up. In addition, you must maintain patience through the struggle. Most importantly, you have to keep your focus, your concentration, and your meditation on the man upstairs. It's only fitting that I leave you with Romans 12:12, which tells us to rejoice in hope, to be patient in tribulation, and to continue steadfastly in prayer.

Words to Live By

Psalm 119

v 49–50: Remember Your word to your servant, in which You have made me hope. This is my comfort in my affliction, that Your promise gives me life.

v 55: I remember Your name in the night, O Lord, and keep Your law.

v 67: Before I was afflicted I went astray, but now I keep Your word.

v 71: It is good for me that I was afflicted, that I might learn Your statutes.

v 77: Let Your mercy come to me, that I may live, for Your law is my delight.

v 92–93: If Your law had not been my delight, I would have perished in my affliction. I will never forget Your precepts, for by them You have given me life.

v 132: Turn to me and be gracious to me, as is Your way with those who love Your name.

v 147–149: I rise before the dawn and cry for help; I hope in Your words. My eyes are awake before the watches of the night that I may meditate on Your promise. Hear my voice according to Your steadfast love; O Lord, according to Your justice give me life.

v 153: Look on my affliction and deliver me, for I do not forget Your law.

About the Author

Gregg Manning was born in 1956 in Memphis, Tennessee, the son of Andy and Frances Manning. From the earliest age, he was introduced to sports, enjoying success in baseball, basketball, football, and golf. The family relocated to Richardson, Texas, a suburb of Dallas, in 1966. He is a graduate of J.J. Pearce High School.

Gregg experienced tennis for the first time in 1968. Ultimately, tennis took him on a great ride, achieving national and international acclaim, including being a collegiate All-American at Northwestern State University in Natchitoches, Louisiana, and a former world-ranked ATP touring professional. Gregg has been a member of the United States Professional Tennis Association since 1981, having directed tennis operations at various tennis clubs around the DFW Metroplex. In addition, the United States Tennis Association chose Gregg as one of America's best coaches in1997. He still trains a select few today.

Gregg got his Texas residential real estate license in 1986. His second career began unsuspectingly on a part-time basis while he was still heavily involved in tennis. In 2001, he hung his license full time with Keller Williams Realty and has never looked back. He is a perennial top producer, having achieved numerous awards and recognitions, including being nominated Best Realtor in Dallas in *D Magazine* and selected as a Five Star Realtor "Best in Client Satisfaction" for *Texas Monthly* magazine 2012, 2013, and 2014. Gregg currently resides in Prosper, Texas, a small community on the north side of Dallas.

Eight months before I was diagnosed

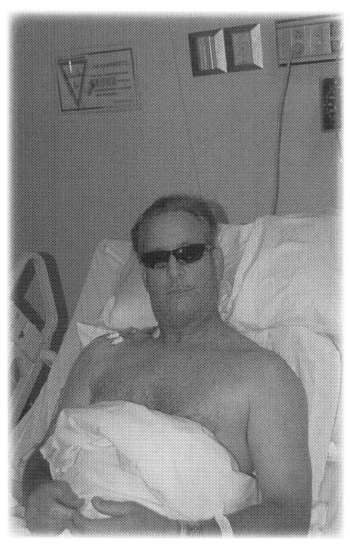

July 3 after the PICC insertion

Francine and Teresa my awesome sisters

The love of my life Marlaine

My four legged daughter Ginger

Today...triumphant